Usborne Workbooks
Spelling

This book belongs to

....

There are answers on page 27, and notes for grown-ups at the back of the book.

Usborne Workbooks
Spelling

Illustrated by Marta Cabrol

Written by Jane Bingham

Designed by Maddison Warnes

You can write in this book and help the animals learn to spell.

At the end of the book there are blank pages for more spelling practice.

Edited by Kristie Pickersgill
Series Editor: Felicity Brooks

Missing letters

The animals are writing labels for their pictures. Can you help them complete their words?

Choose from these starting sounds:

~~tr~~ br cr fl sn

Choose from these ending sounds:

st nt rd nch

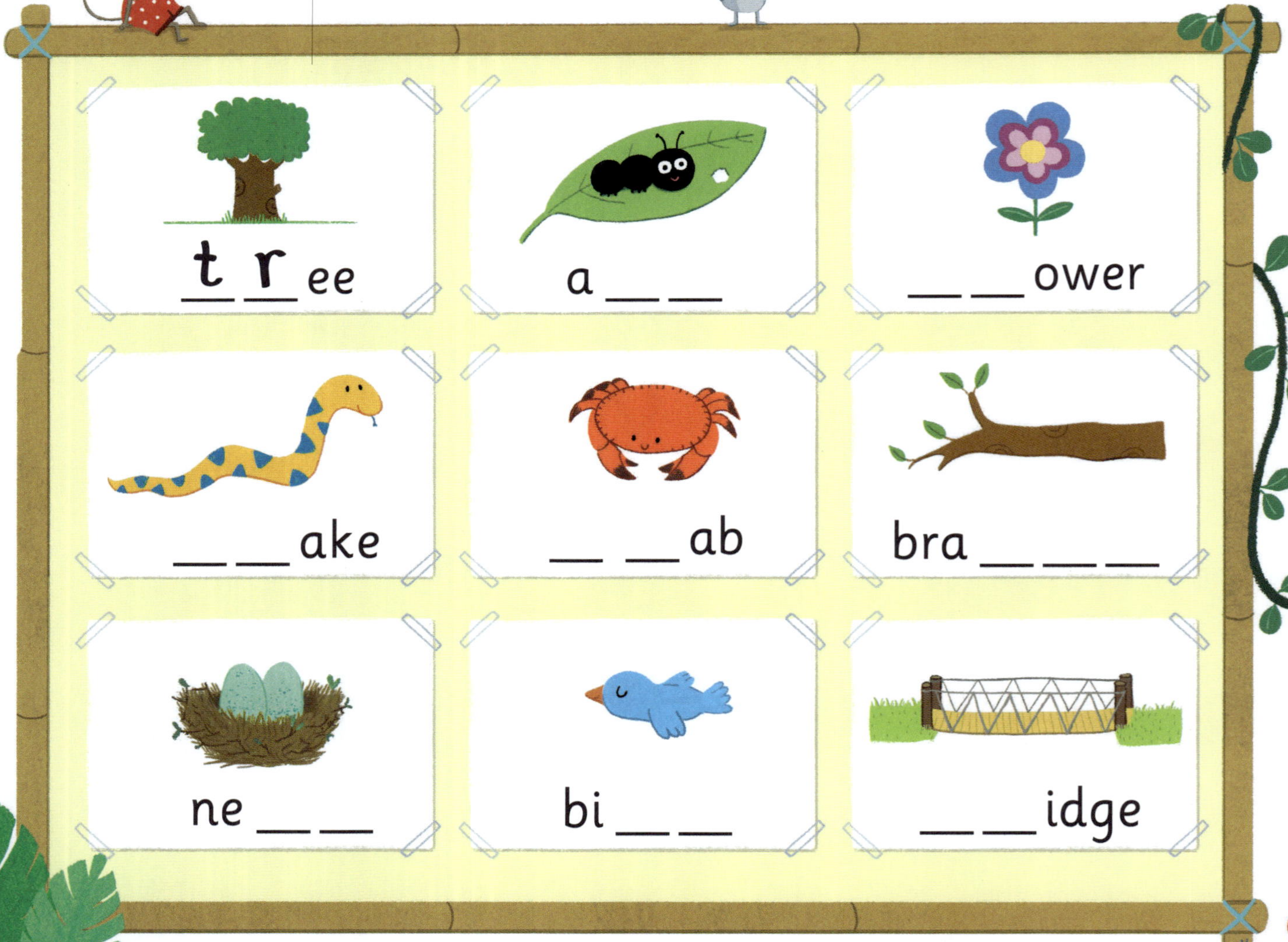

t r ee

a __ __

__ __ ower

__ __ ake

__ __ ab

bra __ __ __

ne __ __

bi __ __

__ __ idge

Don't forget! All these starting and ending sounds are made by blending letter sounds together.

Silent letters

The letters **g** and **k** don't make any sound when they are used in front of **n**, and the letter **w** is silent in front of **r**. Can you draw a ring around six silent letters in Lem's poem?

I wrote a note to Beaky.

It said, 'Please knock, don't gnaw.

You know it's wrong to nibble.

You've wrecked my new front door.'

Ant needs to add a silent **g**, **k** or **w** to complete his words. Look at the pictures and fill in the gaps.

__ nat

__ nee

__ nome

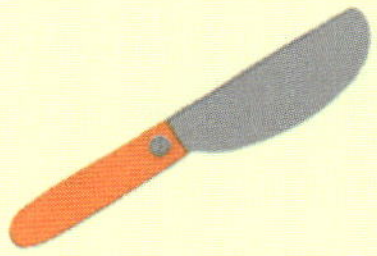

__ nife   __ reath

w k g
g k

When you have used a letter, draw a line through it.

Same sound, different spellings

In some words, the letter **c** makes a **s** sound. Read the sentence in the yellow strip below. Then draw a ring around the letter **c** each time it makes a **s** sound.

The letter c sounds like a s when it goes before e, i or y.

Tig raced through the city on his cousin's bicycle.

Can you choose the right spellings?
Draw a line through the words you think are wrong.

Lem wore a **fansy/fancy** hat.

Baz loves **ice cream/ise cream**.

Lep likes to **danse/dance**.

Cheeky has lost her **pencil/pensil**.

Don't forget!

Remember to check the letter that comes after the c.
If it's e, i or y, the c will sound like s.

The **j** sound can be spelled in several ways. Look at the animals' boards and say their words out loud.

Now complete the words in this story.

One day, Froggy spotted a **g**iant __ar. It was hu__ __! When she peered over the e__ __ __, she saw it was filled with sparkling __ems! Froggy __umped for __oy!

It's magic!

Draw a line through the letters after you have used them.

~~g~~ j dge j
ge j g

Which ending?

Many words end with the letters **le**, but there are other ways to spell this sound. Can you help Cheeky add the right endings to her words?

le or il?

app __ __

foss __ __

le or el?

tow __ __

bott __ __

le or al?

ped __ __

eag __ __

Now read Froggy's story and see if you can spot six places where she's got an ending wrong. Underline the mistakes, then spell the words correctly.

A gerble got into troubel in the middal of a pond. When he tried to paddel, he could only traval backwards! What a strange animil!

g __ __ __ __ __

t __ __ __ __ __ __

m __ __ __ __ __

p __ __ __ __ __

t __ __ __ __ __

a __ __ __ __ __ __

Tig and his friends are learning about words that end in the letters **-ion**. Draw a ring around the words that end in **-sion**. Draw a box around the words that end in **-tion**.

Short words often end in -tion.

There aren't any clear rules for adding -tion or -sion.

You just need lots of spelling practice!

action   decision   conversation
discussion   station   illusion

Can you add **-tion** or **-sion** to these words?

televi _ _ _ _

inven _ _ _ _

man _ _ _ _

rela _ _ _ _

divi _ _ _ _

posi _ _ _ _

Help me finish my words.

Check on page 27 to see how well you've done.

Adding endings

When you add the endings **-ed**, **-ing**, **-er** or **-est** to a word, you sometimes need to make a spelling change. Look at what happens to words that end in **e**.

Drop the letter e before you add an ending.

like + ed = liked
like + ing = liking
safe + er = safer
safe + est = safest

Can you help Froggy make her spelling changes? Write the new words on her raft.

large + er = ...
smile + ing = ...
nice + est = ...
hope + ed = ...

If a word ends with a single short vowel followed by a single consonant, you need to change its spelling when you add an ending.

Can you fill in the gaps in this story? Remember to follow the spelling rule on this page.

run + ing

Tig and Tan-tan had a __ __ __ __ __ __ __

fit + est

race to see who was the __ __ __ __ __ __ __.

jog + ed

Tan-tan __ __ __ __ __ __ as fast as she

win + er

could, but Tig was the __ __ __ __ __ __.

Don't forget!

The five vowels are a, e, i, o and u. All the other letters are consonants.

Adding y

The animals are learning what happens when they add the letter **y** to a word. Look at what they've found out. Then help Crock fill in his weather chart.

If a word ends in e, drop the e.

For most words, just add y.

dirt + y = dirty
shine + y = shiny
spot + y = spotty

For words with a single short vowel followed by a single consonant, double the consonant.

Use the words below to help you complete Crock's chart. Each word on the chart should end in **y**.

| wind | ice | sun | fog | rain | haze |

 sun ___    fog ___

 ic ___   haz ___

 wind ___   rain ___

 **Don't forget!** The five vowels are a, e, i, o and u. All the other letters are consonants.

Watch out for y!

You usually add the letter **s** to make a word plural. But if a word ends in **y**, you sometimes need to make more spelling changes.

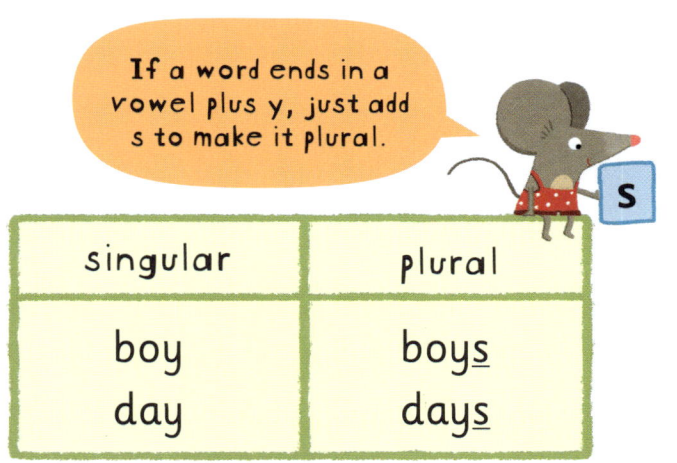

If a word ends in a vowel plus y, just add s to make it plural.

singular	plural
boy	boys
day	days

If a word ends in a consonant plus y, change the y to i, then add –es.

singular	plural
baby	babies
story	stories

Can you help Lem turn her words into plurals?

singular	plural
key	k _ _ _
fly	f _ _ _ _
cherry	c _ _ _ _ _ _ _

The rule for changing **y** to **ies** works for verbs too. Draw a line through the words you think are wrong.

Cheeky always crys/cries when Tan-tan plays/plaies the flute. Then she drys/dries her eyes and says/saies, "I need some fruit!"

Singular means just one of something. Plural means more than one.

More endings

You can change the meaning of some words by adding the endings **-ful, -ment, -ness** or **-less**. Help the animals change their words, but watch out for words that end in **y** and have two syllables (or beats).

Most words don't change when you add an ending.

Words with one syllable that end in y stay the same.

pain + ful = painful
joy + ful = joyful
beauty + ful = beautiful

If a word has two syllables and ends in y, the y changes to i.

Baz is adding endings to his words. Can you help him?

happy + ness = ...

care + ful = ...

penny + less = ...

pay + ment = ...

plenty + ful = ...

Adding -ly

Froggy is adding **-ly** to her words.
Look at what happens to the words.
Then fill in the gaps in her letter.

Most words don't change.

Words that end in y but have one syllable usually stay the same

bad + ly = badly
shy + ly = shyly
easy + ly = easily

If a word ends in y and has two syllables, you need to change the y to i.

Dear Baz,

slow + ly

My friends came to lunch today. Ant ate _____ ,

messy + ly   quick + ly

Tig ate _____ and Crock ate _____ .

happy + ly

Then we all played _____ together!

Love from Froggy

Two words into one

You can make new words by squashing two words together and missing out some letters. These new words are called contractions. The animals are learning how to spell them.

two words	contraction
it + is	it's
they + are	they're

The apostrophe shows the position of the missing letter.

Apostrophes look like commas lifted higher up.

The contraction 'won't' is unusual as it is made from 'will not'. Can you help Ant match the rest of these contractions to the words they were made from?

won't	I am
we're	does not
she'd	will not
can't	we are
wasn't	let us
I'm	she had
let's	can not
doesn't	was not

Lem and her friends are turning two words into one. Can you help them?

do not   **don't**

she will

we have

are not

he is

did not

When you have used a contraction, draw a line through it.

~~don't~~ he's aren't she'll didn't we've

Now fill in the gaps below. Choose from the contractions on the cave wall.

__ __ __ lost my way!

__ __ feeling scared!

__ __ __ all right.

__ __ __ look after you.

It's   I'll   I'm   I've

Don't forget! You often use contractions when you are writing down the words that somebody said.

Who does it belong to?

If you want to show that something belongs to someone, you add an apostrophe plus the letter **s** to the end of their name.

This is called a possessive.

Lem's cap.

The animals are looking for lost clothes. Can you add a possessive (an apostrophe plus the letter **s**) to each of their sentences?

Tan-tan__ shoes are lost.

Is this Ant__ sock?

Where are Crock__ gloves?

Now try shortening these sentences by using a possessive.

These are the boots that belong to Lep.

These are .... boots.......

Cheeky has taken the scarf that belongs to my dad.

Cheeky has taken my........................... scarf....

Using apostrophes

You use an apostrophe to show that letters are missing or to show that something belongs to someone. Look at pages 16 to 18 to remind yourself how to use them. Then, add seven apostrophes to Tan-tan's report.

Add one apostrophe to each line.

Remember! Not all words that end in s need an apostrophe!

Tigs team played brilliantly.

Ive never seen better runners.

Crocks marking was amazing.

Ants goals were fantastic.

The crowd loved Bazs headers.

Were so proud of our team.

Its been a wonderful day!

Getting apostrophes right

Baz sometimes adds an apostrophe when it isn't needed. Draw a ring around two apostrophes that are correct and draw a line through two that shouldn't be there.

Look at Beaky's reminder at the bottom of the page about when you use 'it's'.

It's fun to dress up.

Tan-tan loves glove's.

Look at Cheeky's bag!

The mouse has a bow on it's tail.

Crock's apostrophes are in the wrong position in the words below. Can you write out the words with the apostrophe in the right place?

Crock has'nt seen Tig.

h _ _ _ _

Eeek!

Cheeky ca'nt stop!

c _ _ _

There goes Leps' hat.

L _ _ _

Don't forget!

You only use an apostrophe in the word 'it's' when it is short for 'it is' or 'it has'.

Same sound, different spellings

Some words, such as 'won' and 'one', sound the same but have different spellings and different meanings. Can you help Tan-tan pick the right word from the list to fill the gaps in the sentences?

blew/blue
son/sun
hear/here
be/bee
bear/bare
there/their/they're
sea/see
to/too/two

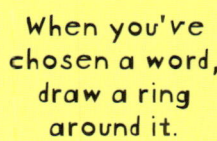

When you've chosen a word, draw a ring around it.

The sky is b _ _ _ and the s _ _ is shining.

I can h _ _ _ a b _ _ buzzing.

Look at that b _ _ _ over th _ _ _ !

Can you s _ _ one bird or t _ _ ?

Check on page 27 to see how well you've done.

Words that sound the same but have a different spelling and a different meaning are called homophones.

Cheeky's signs

Cheeky is writing signs, but she needs some help. Can you add the right endings to her words? When you have used a spelling, draw a line through it. The first one has been done for you.

Turn to page 27 to check your answers. If you want another try, you could use the space on page 28 to have another go.

-old   -ath   -ast
-ass   -ove   -alk

H o l d the handrail!

M _ _ _ very slowly.

Don't go too f _ _ _.

W _ _ _, don't run!

Keep off the gr _ _ _!

Stay on the p _ _ _.

Lep's letter

Can you help Lep choose the right spellings for her letter? Draw a line through the words you think are wrong.

You can look back through the book for spelling help.

Deer/Dear Crock,

I am **riting/writing** to thank you for **one/won** of the best **partys/parties** ever!

I loved your **mums'/mum's giant/jiant** cake. It was **biger/bigger** than the **tabel/table**!

It was so **exsiting/exciting** to **see/sea** your **beautyful/beautiful** river. I **ca'nt/can't** wait to go **swiming/swimming** again!

Love from
Lep

Spelling quiz

Find out how much you can remember about spelling by doing this quiz. The answers are on page 26.

1. Froggy has muddled up her letters. Draw a line to join the start of each word to the right ending. Then write out the words.

   a) kn   ab   ....
   b) gn   ake   ....
   c) sn   ite   ....
   d) wr   aw   ....
   e) cr   ee   ....

2. Can you help Cheeky add endings to these words?

   a) dance + ing = ...
   b) slime + y   = ...
   c) hot   + est = ...
   d) write + er   = ...

3. Tan-tan wants to change singular words into plurals. Can you help her?

   singular   plural

   a) day   ....
   b) box   ....
   c) spy   ....
   d) berry   ....
   e) monkey   ....
   f) hutch   ....

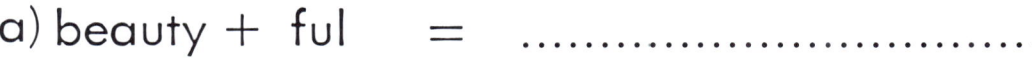

4. Can you help Baz spell new words by adding -ful, -ness and -less?

   a) beauty + ful = ...
   b) hope + less = ...
   c) happy + ness = ...
   d) sad + ness = ...
   e) pity + less = ...
   f) play + ful = ...

5. Ant needs to match these contractions to the words they were made from. Draw a line to match up each pair.

   a) they've   he is
   b) won't   he had
   c) wasn't   they are
   d) he'd   will not
   e) they're   was not
   f) he's   they have

Don't forget that 'won't' is made from 'will not'.

6. Lep's letter is missing seven apostrophes. Can you add them in the right places?

Were having a miserable time. It hasnt stopped raining all week. Dads lost his hat. I cant find my coat. All Mums clothes are soaking and she wont go out. Weve had enough and we want to go home.

7. Look at the picture clues.
   Then spell the words to complete the crossword.

ACROSS

1.  2.

4.

DOWN

1.

2.

3.

Quiz answers

1. a) knee b) gnaw c) snake d) write e) crab
2. a) dancing b) slimy c) hottest d) writer
3. a) days b) boxes c) spies d) berries e) monkeys f) hutches
4. a) beautiful b) hopeless c) happiness d) sadness e) pitiless f) playful
5. a) they've = they have b) won't = will not c) wasn't = was not d) he'd = he had
   e) they're = they are f) he's = he is
6. We're having a miserable time. It hasn't stopped raining all week. Dad's lost his hat. I can't find my coat. All Mum's clothes are soaking and she won't go out. We've had enough and we want to go home.
7. ACROSS 1. keys 2. bridge 4. bicycle
   DOWN   1. knife 2. branch 3. gnome

Score 1 point for each correct answer and write your score in this box: / 40

Answers

Pages 4-5
tree, ant, flower,
snake, crab, branch,
nest, bird, bridge

wrote, knock, gnaw, know, wrong, wrecked
gnat, knee, gnome, knife, wreath

Pages 6-7
ra(c)ed (c)ity bi(c)ycle

Correct spellings:
fancy, ice cream, dance, pencil
giant, jar, huge, edge, gems, jumped, joy

Pages 8-9
apple, fossil, towel, bottle, pedal, eagle
gerbil, trouble, middle, paddle, travel, animal

Words ending -sion: decision, discussion, illusion
Words ending -tion: action, conversation, station

television, invention, mansion,
relation, division, position

Pages 10-11
larger, smiling, nicest, hoped
running, fittest, jogged, winner

Pages 12-13
sunny, foggy, icy, hazy, windy, rainy

keys, flies, cherries
Correct spellings: cries, plays, dries, says

Pages 14-15
happiness, careful, penniless, payment, plentiful
slowly, messily, quickly, happily

Page 16
won't = will not
we're = we are
she'd = she had
can't = can not
wasn't = was not
I'm = I am
let's = let us
doesn't = does not

Page 17
do not = don't
she will = she'll
we have = we've
are not = aren't
he is = he's
did not = didn't

I've, I'm, It's, I'll

Pages 18-19
Tan-tan's, Ant's, Crock's
Lep's, dad's

Tig's, I've, Crock's, Ant's, Baz's, We're, It's

Pages 20-21
Correct words: It's, Cheeky's
Incorrect words: glove's, it's
Correct apostrophes: hasn't, can't, Lep's

blue, sun, hear, bee, bear, there, see, two

Pages 22-23
Hold, Move, fast, Walk, grass, path

Correct spellings: Dear, writing, one, parties, mum's, giant, bigger, table, exciting, see, beautiful, can't, swimming

Don't worry if you made some mistakes. You can rub or cross out your answers and try again.

You can use these pages for writing practice.

Notes for grown-ups

Missing letters/Silent letters (pages 4-5)
The activities on page 4 provide practice in recognizing consonant blends.
On page 5, children are introduced to 'silent letters' in the spellings gn, kn and wr.

Same sound, different spellings (pages 6-7)
Here, children are given guidance and practice in using the soft c sound. They also learn to choose between three different spellings for the j sound.

Which ending? (pages 8-9)
These pages provide practice in choosing between the endings -le, -il, -el and -al, and between the suffixes -tion and -sion.

Adding endings (pages 10-11)
These pages introduce some rules for adding the suffixes -ed, -ing, -er and -est to a root word, and provide practice in implementing those rules. Page 10 covers root words ending in e. Page 11 covers root words ending in a single vowel followed by a single consonant.

Adding y/Watch out for y! (pages 12-13)
Page 12 introduces the spelling rules for adding y to a noun in order to change it into an adjective. Page 13 shows how to form the plural for words ending in a consonant plus y. It also shows how the same spelling rule is used for verbs ending in y.

More endings/Adding -ly (pages 14-15)
Page 14 introduces the spelling rules for adding the suffixes -ful, -ment, -ness and -less.
Page 15 covers the rules for adding -ly to an adjective in order to turn it into an adverb.

Two words into one (pages 16-17)
Here, children are introduced to contractions and are shown how to use apostrophes to indicate missing letters. They are provided with practice in recognizing and forming contractions.

Who does it belong to?/Using apostrophes (pages 18-19)
Page 18 demonstrates the most common way to form a possessive with a singular noun, and provides practice in creating possessives. On page 19, children are encouraged to spot missing apostrophes in contractions and possessives, and to add apostrophes in the correct places.

Getting apostrophes right/Same sound, different spellings (pages 20-21)
Page 20 helps children become more aware of the correct use of apostrophes. Page 21 covers homophones (words that sound the same but have different spellings and meanings, e.g. hear/here).

Cheeky's signs/Lep's letter (pages 22-23)
Page 22 provides practice in spelling some common 'exception words' (ones which are exceptions to the usual spelling rules). Page 23 revises the spellings covered in this book.